THE
ULTIMATE
SALAI
DRESSIN
BOOK

Happy Birthday
Stuart

lots of love
Hil x

THE
ULTIMATE
SALAD
DRESSING
BOOK

CLAIRE STANCER

McGRAW-HILL BOOK COMPANY

New York St. Louis San Francisco

THE ULTIMATE SALAD DRESSING BOOK

Copyright © Claire Stancer, 1988.

All rights reserved. No part of this publication may be reproduced, stored in a data base or retrieval system, or transmitted, in any form or by any means, electronic, mechanical, photocopying, recording, or otherwise, without the prior written permission of McGraw-Hill Ryerson Limited.

ISBN 0-07-549598-8

1234567890 W 7654321098

Cover photography by Steve Lawrence

Illustrations by Brent Mason

Printed and bound in Canada

LIBRARY OF CONGRESS CATALOGING-IN-PUBLICATION DATA

Stancer, Claire.
The ultimate salad dressing book.

Includes index.
1. Salad dressing. I. Title.
TX819.S24S76   1989   641.8'14   88-9118
ISBN 0-07-549598-8

Care has been taken to trace ownership of any copyright material contained in this text. The publishers will gladly take any information that will enable them to rectify any reference or credit in subsequent editions.

CONTENTS

ACKNOWLEDGEMENTS

Special thanks to recipe tester Karen Tufford-Brehn for all her hard work, to my little friend Binkie who greeted me with a big smile every time I came by with more recipes, and to nutritionist Anna Defina for working out the calorie counts for the low-calorie recipes.

Thanks to all my friends who helped so much by tasting, tasting, and tasting ... then offering their inspiring words of wisdom; to Janice Tufford and my dad for all their last-minute help in bringing the book together.

Extra special thanks to my editor, Denise Schon, who made this dream a reality.

INTRODUCTION

People are eating more salads than ever, for a number of reasons. Quick and easy to prepare, salads are an excellent source of vitamins, minerals, nutrients, and fiber. Salads are wholesome, fresh, light, lively, and diverse; a study in contrasts, colors, and textures. A salad can be a complement to a meal, or a meal in itself. Salads are the perfect food for our health-conscious, action-packed way of life. And with more and more people eating more and more salads, we need new and exciting dressings.

With this in mind, I began asking questions about salad dressings. What are the different kinds of dressings? How do they transform a simple salad into something simply delicious? When do you want a creamy dressing, and when a zesty, piquant one? What goes into a basic oil and vinegar dressing? Can I make my own flavored vinegars and oils? Which dressing complements which salad greens? Which dressing goes best with a fruit salad? A seafood salad? Or a meat salad? The more I experimented in my kitchen, the more I came to realize that it's the salad dressing that makes the salad come alive. A salad without a dressing is like a garden without flowers, a canoe without a paddle, wind without trees, a wall without a painting ....

A salad and its dressing must suit each other and make a good "marriage." They must bind together and work together. And like all marriages, the combination can be warm at times and chilly at others, sometimes light and sometimes heavy, sometimes very simple and sometimes very complicated. The union can be sweet or bitter, bland or tart, vital or gentle, wholesome or saucy, and sometimes all of these things at once! A delicious salad depends on its dressing — like two partners who conspire to bring out the best in each other.

In this book I have tried to include every imaginable salad dressing from the classic oil and vinegar to the exotic and adventuresome spicy Hoisen. I have chosen recipes from different cultures and for different tastes, a task made easy because of the availability of exotic greens, oils, vinegars, spices, and herbs in today's food markets. The book is divided into eight major sections: oils, vinegars, vinaigrettes, mayonnaises, dairy-based dressings, warm dressings, low-calorie dressings, and fruit salad dessert dressings. At the beginning, I have included some information on salad greens, herbs, and edible flowers to help you find some new and exciting ingredients for your salads.

Every salad dressing requires a little of the one ingredient that only you can provide — imagination. As you try these recipes, feel free to adjust the vinegar or the sweetness to suit your taste, or to experiment with the textures and varieties of salad greens. Chances are you will develop a new and exotic salad dressing of your very own. This book is just the beginning.

Bon appétit!

SALAD
GREENS

HEAD
LETTUCES

There are three varieties of head lettuce: butterhead, crisp head, and hydroponic.

BUTTERHEAD

BIBB Also known as Kentucky Limestone, Bibb is considered the star of the butterheads. Named after the Kentuckian who developed it, Bibb is smaller than Boston lettuce, but it's the four-star choice.

BOSTON This is the American name for the larger of the two butterheads. It has a fragile head with soft, loosely clustered, crinkled, whitish-green leaves that form a rosette. The butter-sweet, subtle flavor of Boston lettuce is prized by connoisseurs.

Both butterheads are easily perishable.

CRISP HEAD

ICEBERG This is North America's favorite lettuce. Its head is round and firm. Its leaves are pale and bland tasting, and it has a long storage life. Its origins date back to Babylonian times, but its popularity grew in Europe in the sixteenth century, when it was one of the first vegetables planted in every colony (including North America).

HYDROPONIC

This lettuce is specially grown in a strip of plastic foam. A beautiful, soft, green lettuce, it has very little flavor.

LEAF
LETTUCES

Leaf lettuces are most like their wilder ancestors. Unlike their sophisticated cousins, they do not form heads. The color of their leaves ranges from light to dark green; some even have red-tipped leaves. There are three varieties: loose leaf lettuce, romaine, and stem lettuce.

LOOSE LEAF LETTUCE

This name is given to a large group of loose-headed lettuces that are sold under many names. The most popular of these lettuces are the red-tipped and green varieties, with their pretty, frilled edges. These lettuces have a fairly fragile but crisp texture and delicate flavor. Unfortunately, they do not keep well. Other varieties of loose-headed lettuces are oak leaf and red salad bowl.

GREEN LEAF This is also called salad bowl lettuce.

RED LEAF This is the red-tipped member of the leaf lettuce family. It has a crisp but fragile texture and delicate flavor. It is also known as oak leaf lettuce.

ROMAINE

Also known as cos, romaine is one of the most ancient lettuces. Named after the Mediterranean island of Kos, it was very popular in Rome. It is not a true leaf lettuce, but rather a distinctive type. Its feather-shaped green leaves grow in a loose cylinder. Each leaf has a thick midrib, a crisp texture, and a very slight hint of bitterness.

STEM LETTUCE

This unusual and rare lettuce, grown for its crunchy main stem, is cultivated mostly by the Chinese. It is also called woochu or asparagus lettuce.

OTHER GREENS

ARUGULA

Also known as rocket, this is an esteemed Italian green from the mustard family. It is achieving new popularity and receiving rave reviews in North America. It has a pungent, peppery taste which is somewhat milder in the younger, smaller leaves. It works best in a combination with blander greens like Boston, Bibb, or leaf lettuces. Most plentiful in the summer months, it is absent for a time in the winter.

BEET GREENS

The flavor of beet greens resembles a combination of beets and spinach. The younger leaves with their bright green or red streaks make a colorful addition to a salad with other greens, or they can be used on their own with a sweeter Honey Raspberry or Orange Poppyseed Dressing. This green is available from June to October.

CABBAGE

The many varieties of cabbage are included in one form or another in most cuisines. In North America, cabbage is inexpensive and available year round. In the United States, the best seller is the smooth green. Another favorite is the red cabbage with its beautiful purple leaves. The savoy cabbage has a looser head with ruffled leaves, and the Chinese cabbage has green and white leaves that grow in stalks. Kale, another member of the cabbage family, is increasingly popular in North American kitchens.

CHICORY

A close cousin of the endive, this plant grows wild in Europe, Asia, and North America and is usually harvested in July and August. Grown commercially for its root, which is used as a coffee substitute, the flavorful, slightly bitter green adds an interesting taste to any combination salad.

DANDELION GREENS

These are a perfect addition to a salad. The tart, slightly bitter flavor is best in the younger, more tender leaves. Dandelion greens are perfect as a salad addition or on their own with Warm Bacon Dressing.

ENDIVE

BELGIAN ENDIVE It is also known as French endive and wiltloof chicory. It has a compact, bullet-shaped head about 5 inches (13 cm) long. It is grown underground to preserve its creamy white color, which makes it one of the most expensive greens. It has a slightly bitter flavor. Belgian endive is available from September through May.

CURLY ENDIVE Also known as chicory and Frisée, it has a slim, frilled-edge leaf on a loose head. This green has a slightly bitter but pleasant flavor. It is best from late summer through the winter months.

ESCAROLE Distinguished from the other endives by its broad, flat, dark green leaves and its loose head, it has a slightly bitter flavor that works well in a wilted salad with a warm dressing. It is available from late summer through the winter months.

MACHE

Mache is the usual French name for the green that is also known as lamb's quarters, corn salad, or field salad. It is exceedingly popular in France. In North America, it can be found growing wild year round but is most prized in the winter months. The small, dark green leaves have a wonderful nutty flavor.

MUSTARD GREENS

There are several varieties of this green. They have a pungent flavor with a mustardy aftertaste, which works best in a combination with other, gentler-tasting leaves. The younger plants are best and are available in the winter months.

RADICCHIO

It is also called Verona chicory and Tallarosa. Prized by the Italians, this green is grown in the Dolomites and in Verona, Italy. Its smallish head of beautiful purplish-red leaves has a pungent but bitter aftertaste and a slightly chewy texture.

SORREL

Also known as sour grass or dock, this green is similar to spinach with a lemon-flavored tang. The older the leaf, the more pronounced the taste. It is an unusual addition to a combination green salad.

SPINACH

It is a mild-tasting green with a faintly musky flavor and coarse texture. It is available year round and is always a nice addition to a salad.

WATERCRESS

This peppery member of the mustard family perks up a combination salad beautifully. It tastes a little hot, but actually cools and quenches the mouth. A long, tender stem with crisp, deep green leaves, this vegetable can be found year round, but is easily perishable.

HERBS

Savory, sweet, refreshing, or bitter, pot herbs come in a dizzying number. Most have been used since the dawn of civilization in the name of love, religion, medicine, mysticism — and nowadays in salads or salad dressings.

BASIL

There are many varieties including bush, wild, and lemon-scented. Their aromatic scent and taste are perfectly suited to salad and blend especially well with tomatoes.

CHERVIL

A soft, gentle-flavored herb. Chervil is suited to a delicate salad or dressing.

CHIVE

A milder tasting cousin of the onion.

CORIANDER

Sometimes known as cilantro or Chinese parsley, this unusual tasting herb is an essential in Mexican, Indian, or Peruvian cooking.

DILL

Dill's springlike refreshing taste is well suited to fish, cucumber, and potato salads or any yogurt or sour cream dressing.

MARJORAM

The sweet, winter, and pot varieties are all cultivated for kitchen use. This herb is often associated with poultry stuffing, but the fresh, sweet leaves are great in salad flavorings.

MINT

Peppermint, spearmint, orange mint, and other varieties are a welcome addition to your salads. They combine well with potatoes, carrots, peas, grains, or lamb salads; or add it to yogurt for a refreshing dressing.

OREGANO

Oregano combines well with tomatoes, summer squash, or in a simple vinaigrette for a Greek-type salad.

PARSLEY

Don't relegate this misunderstood herb to the side of the plate as a garnish. Both the curly and Italian flat leaf varieties are a wonderful addition to any salad or dressing.

ROSEMARY

There are two varieties of this perfumy herb — a silver and a gold. It has an overwhelming flavor and should be used with some restraint. It's a marvelous complement to any beef, poultry, or seafood salad.

SUMMER SAVORY

The strongly aromatic leaves are a wholesome addition to any leafy salad and are perfect for an herb-flavored vinegar.

TARRAGON

A perennial aromatic herb, which is often combined with chives and chervil, tarragon is frequently used in this combination as a salad flavoring. It also makes a wonderful herb vinegar.

THYME

The lemon, orange, or caraway varieties of thyme give an especially nice, bitter fragrance to your salad.

EDIBLE FLOWERS

A petal of beauty offers a new turn to salads.

BASIL FLOWERS

Like the herb itself, the aromatic white or lavender flowers are a natural complement to any salad.

CHIVE FLOWERS

Surprisingly more pungent than the herb itself.

GERANIUMS

Try all varieties: rose, nutmeg, lemon, and apple geranium blooms and leaves.

HYSSOP

The blue, white, or red flowers lend a refreshing beauty.

LAVENDER

Both the leaves and the lavender colored flowers offer an interesting, almost pungent flavor.

LOVAGE

The frilled leaves, which resemble celery, and the yellow umbels add an almost ornamental touch.

MARIGOLDS

A golden salad garnish, the orange and yellow flowers have been eaten over the centuries.

NASTURTIUM

Flowers, seeds, leaves — all can be used as salad flavorings.

ROSE PETALS

The stronger the aroma, the more flavorful the petal.

VIOLETS

These delicate flowers have been candied and cherished for years as an expensive cake garnish. Try the leaves and the pink and violet blooms with your greens.

ZUCCHINI FLOWERS AND PUMPKIN BLOSSOMS

Traditionally, both these flowers have been stuffed, sautéed in olive oil, or deep fried. They do, however, make a beautiful salad garnish.

ONE

OILS

The foundation of a good dressing lies in the aroma of the oil.
This section describes the different types of oils and offers
some recipes for flavored oils.

THE DIFFERENT
TYPES

CORN OIL

A good, general-purpose oil, corn oil is mild tasting.

COTTONSEED OIL

One of North America's most used oils (usually combined in vegetable oils), cottonseed oil is a mild-tasting, unassuming oil. Other seed oils with similar properties are grapeseed and sunflower seed oils.

OLIVE OIL

Like fine wines, olive oils are affected by the soil in which the trees are grown. Fine olive oils are produced in France, Italy, Spain, and Greece. The color can vary from a light gold to a pale green, depending on the olive.

The higher quality oils are from the first cold pressing. Oils labeled "first pressing virgin," "cold pressing virgin," or "extra virgin" (*vierge*) are the best choice for salads. The subsequent pressings produce a more pungent tasting, inferior oil, and they are labeled "virgin oil," "fine," or "extra fine."

PALM-NUT OIL

This reddish-orange oil has a very characteristic flavor and is used in Brazilian and West African food.

PEANUT OIL

American peanut oil is quite bland, while Chinese peanut oil has a much stronger, nuttier flavor. Both make good additions to light salad dressings and are particularly good oils to use in making mayonnaise.

SAFFLOWER OIL

High in polyunsaturates, this oil is great for those worried about cholesterol. It first became popular because people believed it could magically melt away fat. An unassertive oil, it is best used in light-flavored dressings.

SESAME OIL

The light colored sesame oil is pressed from the raw sesame seed, while the darker variety is pressed from the toasted seed. It gives a nutty flavor to dressings but should be used in combination with other oils because of its strong flavor.

WALNUT OIL

An excellent addition to most salad dressings, walnut oil is ideal for use with the more pungent greens. The rich-tasting, cold-pressed oil is usually imported from the Perigord in France. Walnut oil found in your local health food store tends to be lighter in taste. It has a short shelf life and must be refrigerated in hot weather. Other nut oils include almond, hazelnut, hickory nut, and beech nut. They all must be kept cool in hot weather.

BASIL
OIL

Yield: Approximately 1¹/₂ quarts (1.5 L)

A perfect gift.

2 cups	tightly packed basil leaves, washed and dried	500 mL
1¹/₂ quarts	olive oil	1.5 L
4	fresh basil leaves for garnish	4

1 Place basil leaves in an enamel crock or glass jar. Pour oil over leaves. Cover and steep for 5 to 7 days.

2 Strain oil through a cheesecloth, pressing basil leaves lightly to extract flavors.

3 Place basil leaves in each of 2 clean 3-cup (750 mL) wine bottles. Pour in the strained oil. Cork bottles and store in a cool, dark place.

Try drizzling some basil oil over a salad of freshly harvested, sliced tomatoes, alternated with fresh mozzarella and thinly sliced red onion rings.

VARIATION

THYME OIL Substitute 2 cups (500 mL) fresh thyme for the 2 cups (500 mL) basil leaves. Garnish with 1 medium sprig thyme per bottle.

ORIENTAL
CHILI OIL

Yield: Approximately 1 cup (250 mL)

This spicy seasoning is available in most Chinese markets, but it's easy to make yourself.

1 cup	peanut oil	250 mL
¼ cup	dried chili flakes	50 mL

1 In a small heavy saucepan, heat oil over medium-high heat to 250°F (121°C), or until it is hot enough to bubble up slowly around a chili flake.
2 Add chili flakes, stir to distribute, and set aside until cool.
3 Pour mixture into a clean, dry crock or glass jar and allow to steep for 2 days in a cool, dark place.
4 Strain through cheesecloth into clean bottles, discarding chilies.

The oil will keep for 6 months, and even longer in a cool, dark place.

Ginger root: The ginger root has been around since the time of the ancient Greeks and is a mainstay in Oriental stir frys, desserts, and ginger beers. It keeps best if wrapped in paper and stored in the refrigerator.

VARIATION

GINGER-ORANGE CHILI OIL When adding the chili flakes to the oil, also add 1 inch (2.5 cm) of peeled, thinly sliced ginger, 1 small clove garlic, peeled and lightly smashed, and the grated zest of 1 well-scrubbed orange — about 2½ tablespoons (40 mL). After straining into bottles, for decoration, add 2 chili flakes, 1 clove garlic, and a ½ inch (1.5 cm) piece of ginger before corking.

PROVENÇAL FLAVORED OIL

Yield: Approximately 1½ quarts (1.5 L)

The flavorings in this oil make the sunshine and smells of summer in southern France your very own.

1 cup	large branches fresh rosemary, coarsely chopped	250 mL
10	medium bay leaves, broken	10
4	cloves garlic, lightly smashed	4
2	small chili peppers	2
1½ quarts	olive oil	1.5 L
Garnish:		
¼ cup	pine nuts, toasted	50 mL
2 sprigs	rosemary	2 sprigs
2	bay leaves	2
4	chili peppers	4

1 Place rosemary, bay leaves, garlic, and chili peppers in an enamel crock or glass jar. Pour oil over, cover, and let steep for 12 days.
2 Strain oil through a cheesecloth, pressing rosemary lightly to extract flavor.
3 Place 2 tablespoons (25 mL) pine nuts, 1 sprig rosemary, 1 bay leaf, and 2 chili peppers in each of 2 clean and dry 3-cup (750 mL) wine bottles. Don't forget to label them. Pour in strained oil, cork, and store in a cool, dark place.

ROASTED
PECAN OIL

Yield: Approximately 2 cups (500 mL)

| 1 cup | pecan pieces | 250 mL |
| 2 cups | peanut or cottonseed oil | 500 mL |

1 Preheat oven to 350°F (180°C).
2 Lay pecan pieces on baking sheet and toast until golden brown, about 8 minutes.
3 Meanwhile, in a medium-sized saucepan, heat oil over medium-high heat to 300°F (150°C), or until oil is hot enough to bubble up slowly around a pecan piece.
4 Add pecan pieces, stir to distribute, and set aside to cool.
5 Pour mixture into a clean, dry crock or glass jar and steep for 7 days in a cool, dark place.
6 Strain through cheesecloth into a clean bottle, discarding all but 1 teaspoon (5 mL) roasted pecans. Add to bottle and cork. Store oil in a very cool, dark place or refrigerate.

VARIATIONS

WALNUT OIL Substitute 1 cup walnut pieces for pecans.

HAZELNUT OIL Substitute 1½ cups (375 mL) whole hazelnuts for pecans. After roasting in preheated oven, rub hazelnuts together in a dishcloth to remove skin. Chop nuts coarsely and add to crock or glass jar. Continue as in pecan recipe.

ALMOND OIL Substitute 1½ cups (375 mL) blanched almonds for pecans. Roast in preheated oven and chop coarsely before adding to crock or glass jar. Continue as for pecan recipe.

TWO

VINEGARS

Oil and vinegar are the two most basic ingredients of a salad dressing.

The word *vinegar* stems from the French words *vin* (wine) and *aigre* (sour) or "sour wine." It's so named because the French have traditionally prepared their vinegar from soured wine.

This section provides an introduction to the different types of vinegars and a number of easy recipes for herb, spice, and fruit-flavored vinegars.

THE DIFFERENT
TYPES

These delightfully flavored vinegars will complement your homemade dressings. Most are available in specialty food shops or grocery stores.

BALSAMIC VINEGAR

Also known as Aceto Balsamico, this vinegar is like a fine wine. Its rich, almost sweet flavor is created by a long aging process in wooden barrels. It complements most greens and tastes good when combined with a fine virgin olive oil.

CHAMPAGNE VINEGAR

Most often imported from the Champagne region in France, this vinegar is the fermentation of champagne. It has a sweet and delicate flavor that is best suited for use with lightly flavored foods like mache, seafood, or fruit salads. It works best with a light-flavored oil.

CIDER VINEGAR

Made from the fermentation of apple cider, this vinegar is a standby for an everyday-type dressing. You can taste a hint of the fruit in it.

DISTILLED WHITE VINEGAR

This vinegar tastes rather harsh when used in a dressing but is perfect for pickling or preserving.

LEMON AND LIME JUICES

Vinegar is not the only acidic element used in a dressing. Lemon and lime juices have a delicate flavor best suited to fish or fruit salads.

MALT VINEGAR

Made from a combination of grain and cider vinegar, malt vinegar has a rich, tart flavor that is ideal for a remoulade, tartar sauce, or pungent mustard vinaigrette.

RASPBERRY VINEGAR

This is one of the many fruit-flavored, white wine vinegars. Available in most gourmet shops, they add a nice light touch to any dressing. Among the other fruit vinegars available are blueberry, cassis, strawberry, and pear.

RED WINE VINEGAR

Made from any red wine, this vinegar has a sharp, robust flavor and is best served with the more assertive greens like arugula, romaine, and radicchio or with red meat salads. It combines well with olive oil.

RICE VINEGAR

Chinese rice vinegar is sharper in taste, while the Japanese is a little sweeter and more mellow. Both complement any fish or seafood salad and combine well with peanut and sesame oils.

SHERRY VINEGAR

This vinegar is imported from Spain and made from their famed sherry. Aged in wooden barrels, it is rich and smooth in taste with a slightly tart flavor but sweet aftertaste.

TARRAGON VINEGAR

This is one of the many herb-flavored red or white wine vinegars available at most gourmet markets. Other herb flavors are available, including dill, summer savory, and thyme.

WHITE WINE VINEGAR

Made from a number of different white wines, this vinegar is less assertive than its red counterpart. It melds nicely with sweet, delicate ingredients like mache, Boston or Bibb lettuces, or chicken or fish salads.

CAJUN
VINEGAR

Yield: Approximately 1 quart (1 L)

This vinegar makes a wonderful spicy addition to your favorite salsa.

1 quart	red wine vinegar	1 L
1 tablespoon	coarsely crushed black peppercorns	15 mL
4	jalapeno peppers, quartered	4
2	cloves garlic, lightly crushed	2

1 In a medium-sized enameled (non-metallic) pan, bring vinegar, peppercorns, jalapeno peppers, and garlic just to a boil.
2 Pour into a crock or jar and let steep for 6 days.
3 Strain through a cheesecloth and discard flavorings.
4 Pour strained vinegar into a clean, dry 1-quart (1 L) wine bottle and cork. Store in a cool, dark place.

GARLIC
VINEGAR

Yield: Approximately 1 quart (1 L)

1 quart	cider, malt, red, or white wine vinegar	1 L
1 teaspoon	black peppercorns	5 mL
10	cloves garlic, crushed	10

1 In a medium-sized enameled or other non-metallic saucepan, bring vinegar to a boil over medium heat.
2 Meanwhile, coarsely crush peppercorns with the bottom of a heavy saucepan. Place in a glass or other non-metallic jar. Add garlic.
3 Pour in hot vinegar. Let steep for 7 days.
4 Strain through cheesecloth and pour into a clean 1-quart (1 L) wine bottle. Cork and store in a cool, dark place. Keeps 1 year.

GREEN PEPPERCORN VINEGAR

Yield: Approximately 1 quart (1 L)

| 1 quart | cider or malt vinegar | 1 L |
| 3 tablespoons | crushed peppercorns | 50 mL |

1 In a medium-sized enameled or other non-metallic saucepan, bring vinegar to a boil over medium heat.
2 Meanwhile, coarsely crush peppercorns with the bottom of a heavy saucepan. Place in a glass or non-metallic jar.
3 Pour in hot vinegar. Let steep for 7 days.
4 Strain through cheesecloth and pour into a clean 1-quart (1 L) wine bottle. Cork and store in a cool, dark place. Keeps 1 year.

HERB AND SPICE
VINEGAR

Yield: Approximately 1 quart (1 L)

Spice vinegars may be substituted wherever ordinary vinegar is called for. Plain or fancy, the vinegar adds a flavorful touch to a salad dressing or acts as a base for a more elaborate mayonnaise.

1 quart	cider or malt vinegar	1 L
3 tablespoons	allspice berries	50 mL
3 tablespoons	coriander seeds	50 mL
1 tablespoon	mustard seeds	15 mL
1	cinnamon stick, 3 inches (7.5 cm) long	1
6	whole cloves	6
1	bay leaf	1
1 inch	ginger root, peeled and thinly sliced	2.5 cm

1 In a medium-sized enameled or other non-metallic saucepan, bring vinegar to a boil over medium heat.
2 Meanwhile, with a mortar and pestle or with the bottom of a heavy saucepan, crush allspice berries and coriander seeds. Place in a non-metallic crock. Add mustard seeds, cinnamon, cloves, bay leaf, and ginger root.
3 Pour in hot vinegar. Cover and let steep for 6 days.
4 Strain through cheesecloth and pour into a clean, dry 1-quart (1 L) wine bottle. Cork and store in a cool, dark place.

RASPBERRY VINEGAR

Yield: Approximately 1 quart (1 L)

The fruity flavor adds freshness and a delicate touch to any salad dressing you'll make.

1 quart	white wine vinegar	1 L
2 cups	fresh raspberries	500 mL
2 inch	piece of lemon rind	5 cm
2	raspberries for garnish	2

1 In a medium-sized enameled (non-metallic) saucepan, bring vinegar, raspberries, and lemon rind just to a boil. Pour into a crock or jar and let steep covered for 3 to 5 days.
2 Strain through a cheesecloth, discarding fruit.
3 Place 2 fresh raspberries in the bottom of a clean, dry 1-quart (1 L) wine bottle. Cork and store in a cool, dark place.

VARIATIONS

PEAR VINEGAR Replace raspberries with 2 cups (500 mL) chopped and seeded pears.

STRAWBERRY VINEGAR Replace raspberries with 2 cups (500 mL) hulled and halved fresh strawberries.

BLACK CURRANT VINEGAR Replace raspberries with 2 cups (500 mL) cleaned, slightly crushed black currants.

ROSE VINEGAR

Yield: Approximately ½ quart (500 mL)

1 quart	white wine vinegar	1 L
4 cups	fresh rose petals	1 L
2 inch	piece of lemon rind	5 cm

1 In a medium-sized enameled (non-metallic) saucepan, bring vinegar, rose petals, and lemon rind just to a boil. Pour into a crock or jar and let steep covered for 5 to 7 days.
2 Strain through a cheesecloth, discarding petals.
3 Pour into a clean 3-cup (750 mL) wine bottle. Cork and store in a cool, dark place.

ROSEMARY VINEGAR

Yield: Approximately 2¹/₃ cups (575 mL)

1 quart	cider, malt, red wine, or white wine vinegar	1 L
2 cups	fresh rosemary, bruised	500 mL

1 In a medium-sized enameled or other non-metallic saucepan, bring vinegar to a boil over medium heat.
2 Place rosemary in glass or other non-metallic jar.
3 Pour in hot vinegar. Cover and let steep for 5 days.
4 Pour into a clean 3-cup (750 mL) wine bottle. Cork and store in a cool, dark place.

This herb vinegar combined with a little olive oil and crushed garlic makes a wonderful marinade for grilled fish.

VARIATION

For a different herb-flavored vinegar, replace rosemary with 2 cups (500 mL) dill, mint, basil, tarragon, or thyme.

THREE

VINAIGRETTES

Salads can be traced back to the ancient Greeks and Romans who served dishes made from edible herbs or plants dressed only with salt. In fact, the word *salad* derives from *sal*, the Latin word for salt. Today, salads are made from a wide variety of ingredients: fruits, vegetables, flowers, herbs, meats, cheese, fish, and pasta. They can be cooked or raw, warm or cold, and most are dressed with a vinaigrette – a classic combination of vinegar, oil, salt, and pepper. This section covers a number of vinaigrette recipes from the very traditional to the wonderfully wild.

CLASSIC
VINAIGRETTE

Yield: Approximately ²/₃ cup (150 mL)

1 tablespoon	Dijon-style mustard	15 mL
3 tablespoons	vinegar (red wine, balsamic, cider, or other) or lemon or lime juice	50 mL
¹/₂ cup plus 2 tablespoons	oil (corn, safflower, peanut, or olive) or a combination	125 mL
	Salt	
	Freshly ground white pepper	

1 In a small bowl, whisk together the mustard and the vinegar until well combined.

2 While continuing to whisk, slowly drizzle in a thin stream of oil. Season with salt and pepper to taste. Chill until serving.

Note: Dressing may need to be rewhisked, shaken, or brought back to room temperature before serving.

VARIATIONS

CREAMY VINAIGRETTE Add 1 egg yolk to Classic Vinaigrette recipe. Whisk together with mustard and vinegar. Follow the rest of the Classic Vinaigrette recipe. This version is especially good made with raspberry or blackberry vinegar.

HERB VINAIGRETTE Add 2 tablespoons (25 mL) of mixed, finely chopped parsley, chervil, basil, chives, and tarragon and 1 finely chopped shallot to the Classic Vinaigrette recipe.

ROQUEFORT OR BLUE CHEESE VINAIGRETTE Add ¹/₄ cup (50 mL) Roquefort or blue cheese, 2 tablespoons (25 mL) heavy cream or crème fraîche, and 1 tablespoon (15 mL) walnut oil to the Classic Vinaigrette recipe.

TARRAGON VINAIGRETTE Replace vinegar in Classic Vinaigrette with tarragon vinegar and mustard with tarragon mustard. Add 2 tablespoons (25 mL) finely chopped fresh tarragon or 1 teaspoon (5 mL) dried.

MUSTARD VINAIGRETTE

Yield: Approximately ³/₄ cup (175 mL)

1¹/₂ tablespoons	Dijon-style mustard	20 mL
2 tablespoons	malt vinegar	25 mL
¹/₂ cup	corn or safflower oil	125 mL
1	clove garlic, minced	1
1	shallot, finely diced	1
	Salt	
	Freshly ground white pepper	

1 In a small bowl, whisk together mustard and vinegar until combined.

2 Slowly drizzle in oil while whisking constantly.

3 Stir in garlic and shallot. Season with salt and pepper to taste. For best results, refrigerate 1 to 2 hours to allow for enhancement of flavors.

For a mouth-watering first course, serve this dressing over a combination of curly endive and Boston and Bibb lettuces accompanied by large garlic croutons.

Large Garlic Croutons: Crush 1 large clove garlic with a pinch of salt. Whisk in ¹/₃ cup (75 mL) olive oil. Brush on twelve ¹/₄-inch (0.5 cm) thick slices stale French bread. Bake in a preheated 325°F (160°C) oven until golden, about 15 minutes.

CHEESEY GREEK
SALAD DRESSING

Yield: Approximately ²/₃ cup (150 mL)

Garlic and Parmesan cheese are classic flavormates that make this
dressing truly special.

¹/₄ cup	red wine vinegar	50 mL
¹/₃ cup	corn or safflower oil	75 mL
¹/₂ cup	olive oil	125 mL
2	medium cloves garlic, minced	2
2 drops	Worcestershire sauce	2 drops
¹/₂ tablespoon	dried oregano	7 mL
2 tablespoons	freshly grated Parmesan cheese	25 mL
¹/₄ cup	crumbled feta cheese	50 mL
	Salt	
	Freshly ground black pepper	

1 In bowl of blender or food processor fitted with a steel blade,
   combine vinegar, oils, garlic, Worcestershire sauce, and oregano.
   Process 1 minute, or until smooth, scraping down sides
   occasionally.
2 Stir in Parmesan and feta cheeses and season with salt and pepper
   to taste. Chill until serving.

This dressing is wonderful over crisp lettuce with cucumber and
tomato wedges, red onion, crunchy green pepper rings, and spicy
Greek olives.

*Feta Cheese: Believed to have been developed by shepherds in the
Balkan mountain regions, feta cheese is known as the "pickled cheese"
because it is aged in brine. It can be made from ewe's milk, goat's
milk, or cow's milk. American feta is made from cow's milk and is
quite sharp. Australian feta is slightly salty. Bulgarian is sweet and
creamy. Danish is made from cow's milk and can have quite a harsh
taste. German is sweet and creamy, and Italian feta is drier and
coarser than the rest.*

BLACK BEAN AND TOMATO DRESSING

Yield: Approximately 1¹/₃ cups (325 mL)

The Far East meets the Mediterranean in this exotic combination of Chinese black beans and Italian tomatoes.

3 tablespoons	olive oil	50 mL
2	cloves garlic, minced	2
¹/₂ teaspoon	dried chilies (optional)	2 mL
3	green onions, finely sliced	3
1 inch	ginger, finely grated	2.5 cm
3 tablespoons	dried black beans, chopped	50 mL
2 teaspoons	granulated sugar	10 mL
2 tablespoons	tomato paste	25 mL
2 teaspoons	Dijon-style mustard	10 mL
¹/₄ cup	red wine vinegar	50 mL
¹/₂ teaspoon	sesame oil	2 mL
¹/₂ cup	corn or peanut oil	125 mL
¹/₂ cup	chopped tomatoes (approximately 1 medium)	125 mL
	Salt	
	Freshly ground black pepper	

1 In a medium-sized skillet, heat olive oil over medium heat.

2 Add garlic, chilies, onions, ginger, and black beans. Sauté 2 to 3 minutes, stirring constantly. Remove with slotted spoon to a medium-sized bowl.

3 Whisk in sugar, tomato paste, mustard, and vinegar. Slowly whisk in oils. Stir in tomatoes and season with salt and pepper to taste.

This dressing complements any pasta salad. Toss it over rotini noodles, blanched snow peas and broccoli, or sliced red peppers and steamed, shucked mussels.

Fermented Black Beans: A staple in Chinese cuisine, fermented black beans are black soy beans that have been salted and partially dried to preserve them. Soak the fragrant beans for about 30 minutes in cold water to rid them of excess salt.

HOISEN DRESSING

Yield: Approximately ³/₄ cup (175 mL)

Hoisen sauce adds an exotic, sweet, and smoky flavor that will send your taste buds to the Far East.

2 tablespoons	Hoisen sauce	25 mL
3 tablespoons	Mirin rice wine	50 mL
¹/₄ cup	cider vinegar	50 mL
¹/₃ cup	safflower or peanut oil	75 mL
¹/₄ teaspoon	chili oil	1 mL
1	medium clove garlic, minced	1
	Salt	
	Freshly ground black pepper	

1 In a small bowl, whisk together Hoisen sauce, rice wine, and vinegar until combined.

2 Slowly whisk in oils. Add garlic and season with salt and pepper to taste.

Toss this dressing over a combination of lightly boiled Shanghai noodles, strips of smoked duck or chicken, julienned strips of yellow pepper, shredded leaf lettuce, and sliced yellow, green, and red plums.

Hoisen Sauce: This sweet, spicy, reddish-brown sauce is made from soy beans, garlic, and spices. The Chinese brush it on barbecued meat. It is available in any Chinese grocery store.

Mirin: This Japanese rice wine is sweeter than sake and is used for cooking. It is available in most Chinese grocery stores, or a dry sherry may be used as a substitute.

HONEY RASPBERRY VINAIGRETTE

Yield: Approximately 1 cup (250 mL)

It's so easy to make your own raspberry vinegar (page 28). Now you can use it in this light and elegant fruity dressing.

¹/₄ cup	raspberry vinegar or other fruit vinegar	50 mL
2 tablespoons	honey	25 mL
1 teaspoon	Dijon-style mustard	5 mL
1	small shallot, finely diced	1
²/₃ cup	safflower or corn oil	150 mL
	Salt	
	Freshly ground white pepper	

1 In a small bowl, whisk together vinegar, honey, and mustard until smooth. Add shallot. Continue to whisk mixture while slowly drizzling in oil. Season with salt and pepper to taste. Chill until serving.

This light dressing works well on the butter lettuces — maybe a simple salad of Boston lettuce or Bibb lettuce with some red onion slices?

LEMON CORIANDER DRESSING

Yield: Approximately 1 cup (250 mL)

1	small clove garlic, minced	1
½ cup	olive oil	125 mL
½ cup	safflower or corn oil	125 mL
⅓ cup	lemon juice	75 mL
¼ cup	green onions, finely sliced	50 mL
1 teaspoon	ground coriander	5 mL
1 teaspoon	ground cumin	5 mL
	Salt	
	Freshly ground black pepper	

1 Combine all ingredients in a small bowl. Chill several hours to allow coriander flavor to develop.

This dressing was developed for a tabouleh salad. I make tabouleh by soaking equal parts couscous and mint tea, then adding chopped tomatoes, sliced green onions, lots of chopped parsley and mint, black olives, and salt and pepper. Then I toss it all together with Lemon Coriander Dressing.

MEXICAN–STYLE
SALSA DRESSING

Yield: Approximately 1¹/₄ cups (300 mL)

The fresh cilantro gives this dressing a tantalizing tang.

1	medium clove garlic, minced	1
²/₃ cup	corn or safflower oil	150 mL
¹/₃ cup plus 1 tablespoon	jalapeno vinegar	90 mL
2 tablespoons	finely diced tomato or tomatillo	25 mL
2 tablespoons	chopped cilantro (coriander)	25 mL
1 tablespoon	finely diced Spanish onion	15 mL
1 tablespoon	finely diced green pepper	15 mL
1 tablespoon	finely diced yellow pepper	15 mL
	Salt	
	Freshly ground pepper	
	Cayenne pepper (optional)	

1 Combine all ingredients in a small bowl. Chill at least 1 hour to allow flavors to enhance.

For a Mexican-style corn salad, toss this dressing over blanched corn niblets and add crumbled bacon. Or use on a warm Mexican salad with nacho chips, warmed chili, shredded lettuce, chopped tomatoes, avocado, and shredded Monterey Jack cheese. Or use as a marinade for a seviche of scallops, halibut strips, and shrimp.

Cilantro: Sometimes known as fresh coriander or Chinese parsley, this herb has a distinctive perfume that adds a Mexican, Peruvian, or Indian flavor to any dish. People give it either rave reviews or a definite thumbs down.

MOORLAND HERB
DRESSING

Yield: Approximately ½ cup (125 mL)

This recipe comes from Edinburgh chef David Kerr and contains a wee touch of his Scottish moors.

1½ teaspoons	chopped fresh thyme	7 mL
1 teaspoon	chopped fresh rosemary	5 mL
1 teaspoon	heather or clover honey	5 mL
2½ teaspoons	whole grain mustard	12 mL
1	large egg yolk	1
⅓ cup	peanut oil	75 mL
2 tablespoons	white wine vinegar	25 mL
	Salt	
	White pepper	
	Mace	

1 In bowl of blender or food processor fitted with a steel blade, combine thyme, rosemary, honey, mustard, and egg yolk. Process 10 seconds, or until smooth.

2 With machine running, slowly drizzle in oil until thickened slightly. Stir in vinegar and season with salt, pepper, and mace to taste.

David says that in simple and traditional Scottish fare this dressing is served on a new potato salad as an accompaniment to cold roast lamb.

ORANGE POPPYSEED DRESSING

Yield: Approximately 1¹/₃ cups (325 mL)

²/₃ cup	safflower or corn oil	150 mL
¹/₄ cup	lime juice	50 mL
2 tablespoons	orange juice	25 mL
2 tablespoons	grated orange zest	25 mL
2 tablespoons	honey	25 mL
2 tablespoons	finely diced red onion	25 mL
1 tablespoon	poppy seeds, toasted slightly	15 mL
	Salt	
	Freshly ground black pepper	

1 Place all ingredients in a screw-top jar. Shake vigorously. Chill until serving.

This dressing complements any green salad, but the addition of some small chunks of cantelope, honeydew, or star fruit to your greens will enhance the orange-honey flavor of the dressing. Or try it over slices of cold roast pork with nectarine wedges on watercress.

Poppy Seeds: Did you know that it takes almost a million seeds to make a pound? These tiny bluish-black gems come from the opium poppy plant. But even if you eat a million, you won't experience any narcotic effect. Connoisseurs say those imported from Holland taste best, but for even better flavor, seeds should be toasted slightly in a 350°F (180°C) oven for about 5 minutes.

PORT WALNUT DRESSING

Yield: Approximately 1 cup (250 mL)

This somewhat rarefied dressing was developed by California caterer George Dolese, whose salads are featured at Neiman-Marcus.

¹/₄ cup	port wine	50 mL
2 tablespoons	sherry vinegar	25 mL
2 tablespoons	walnut oil	25 mL
¹/₂ cup	peanut oil	125 mL
	Salt	
	Freshly ground white pepper	

1 In bowl of blender or food processor fitted with a steel blade, combine the port and vinegar. Process 5 seconds.
2 With machine running, slowly drizzle in oils until combined. Season with salt and pepper to taste. Serve at room temperature.

George serves this dressing over a salad of Belgian endive, arugula, radicchio, fresh figs or blanched English snap peas, Stilton cheese, and coarsely chopped walnuts.

QUEBEC OR VERMONT MAPLE VINAIGRETTE

Yield: Approximately 1 cup (250 mL)

1	medium clove garlic, minced	1
²/₃ cup	corn, safflower, or peanut oil	150 mL
¹/₃ cup	cider vinegar	75 mL
¹/₄ cup	Quebec or Vermont maple syrup	50 mL
¹/₂ teaspoon	dry mustard	2 mL
	Salt	
	Freshly ground white pepper	

1 Combine all ingredients in a screw-top jar and shake until well blended.

This dressing will enhance any fruit and greens combination. For something truly unusual, drizzle it over slices of blood oranges and red onions on beet greens.

PESTO SALAD DRESSING

Yield: Approximately 1½ cups (375 mL)

Fresh, sweet-tasting basil is the very essence of a perfect summer harvest.

¾ cup	olive oil	175 mL
⅓ cup	pesto	75 mL
⅓ cup	balsamic vinegar	75 mL
¼ cup	corn or safflower oil	50 mL
¼ cup	pine nuts, walnuts, or almonds, toasted and coarsely chopped	50 mL
	Salt	
	Freshly ground black pepper	

1 Whisk together all ingredients. Chill before serving.

A perfect dressing to pour over thick slices of freshly harvested beefsteak tomatoes. Or toss it over cooled pasta with chunks of chicken and cherry tomatoes.

Pesto: Place 1 cup (250 mL) firmly packed fresh basil, mint, parsley, or summer savory leaves; 1 large clove garlic, minced; ¼ cup (50 mL) pine nuts, walnuts, or blanched almonds; and ¼ cup (50 mL) olive oil in bowl of blender or food processor fitted with a steel blade. Process, scraping down sides occasionally, until smooth. Add ⅓ cup (75 mL) Parmesan cheese and pepper to taste and process for a few seconds more. Store leftovers in the freezer to bring back the flavors of summer in frigid February.

PICKLED GINGER
VINAIGRETTE

Yield: Approximately 1 cup (250 mL)

New York chef and cooking instructor Nancy Newman developed this recipe as part of a Japanese menu she offers in her classes.

¹/₄ cup	balsamic vinegar	50 mL
1 tablespoon	soy sauce	15 mL
¹/₄ cup	olive oil	50 mL
¹/₂ cup	safflower or peanut oil	125 mL
2 tablespoons	sesame oil	25 mL
8 pieces	sweet pickled ginger, finely julienned	8 pieces
	Salt	
	Freshly ground black pepper	

1   In a small bowl, whisk together the vinegar and soy sauce. Slowly whisk in oils and add the ginger. Season with salt and pepper to taste.

Nancy finds that the dressing is perfect for a salad of arugula and red onion; the bitterness of the green and the acidity of the onion contrast nicely with the sweet pickled ginger. She sometimes pickles an assortment of baby vegetables to garnish the salad.

Pickled Baby Vegetables: Bring 3 cups (750 mL) water, ²/₃ cup (150 mL) white sugar, and ¹/₂ cup (125 mL) white wine vinegar to a boil. Add 2 tablespoons (25 mL) pickling spices. Add 4 cups (1 L) assorted baby vegetables such as carrots, pattypan squash, and zucchini. Simmer about 10 minutes. Cool and store in liquid. Drain before serving.

ROASTED RED PEPPER AND CHIVE DRESSING

Yield: 1¹/₂ cups (375 mL)

My good friend, caterer George Dolese, brings out the "real" California taste with this wonderful concoction featured at Neiman-Marcus.

1	medium-sized sweet red pepper or ¹/₂ cup (125 mL) prepared roasted red peppers*	1
¹/₃ cup	red wine vinegar	75 mL
1	medium clove garlic, minced	1
1 cup	olive oil	250 mL
¹/₃ cup	finely chopped fresh chives	75 mL
	Salt	
	Freshly ground white pepper	

1 Hold red pepper over a flame, turning it until evenly charred. Or cut it in half, rub with oil, and place under the broiler until blackened. Wrap in a plastic bag and set aside to cool. Scrape off the burned skin and remove seeds and stem.

2 In bowl of blender or food processor fitted with a steel blade, place red pepper, vinegar, and garlic. Process until pepper is puréed.

3 With machine running, slowly drizzle in olive oil until fully combined. Stir in chives and season with salt and pepper to taste.

George serves this dressing over a salad of fusilli pasta, chunks of fresh mozzarella, julienned zucchini and prosciutto, sliced smoked chicken, and blanched asparagus.

Prepared roasted red peppers are available in jars at Italian specialty stores.

SPICY INDIAN DRESSING

Yield: Approximately 1 cup (250 mL)

Another designer dressing by my friend California caterer George Dolese. Your taste buds won't believe this sensation.

1 tablespoon	Dijon-style mustard	15 mL
¼ cup	rice wine vinegar	50 mL
2 tablespoons	orange marmalade	25 mL
1 tablespoon	honey	15 mL
½ cup	fresh mint leaves, stems removed	125 mL
⅛ teaspoon	ground cloves	0.5 mL
½ teaspoon	ground cinnamon	2 mL
1 teaspoon	ground ginger	5 mL
1 tablespoon	mild curry powder	15 mL
¾ cup	peanut oil	175 mL
¼ cup	mustard oil*	50 mL
	Salt	
	Freshly ground black pepper	

1 In bowl of blender or food processor fitted with a steel blade, combine mustard, vinegar, marmalade, honey, mint, cloves, cinnamon, ginger, and curry powder. Process about 15 seconds, or until smooth.

2 With machine running, slowly drizzle in oils until thickened. Season with salt and pepper to taste and chill until serving.

For a beautiful luncheon, pour this dressing over a cooled poached chicken breast and garnish with orange segments and seedless green grapes.

*Mustard oil is available at Indian grocery stores.

SUN–DRIED TOMATO DRESSING

Yield: Approximately 1²/₃ cups (400 mL)

These tomatoes are in, and it looks as though they're here to stay. But who'd think that a salad dressing could remind you of basking in the sun off the Mediterranean coast.

¹/₂ cup	drained, sun-dried tomatoes packed in oil, finely chopped	125 mL
¹/₂	medium-sized roasted red pepper, peeled, seeds and stem removed (page 48)	¹/₂
1 tablespoon	Dijon-style mustard	15 mL
2	cloves garlic, minced	2
¹/₄ cup	red wine vinegar	50 mL
2 tablespoons	finely chopped red onion	25 mL
³/₄ cup	olive oil	175 mL
¹/₃ cup	corn or safflower oil	75 mL
	Salt	
	Freshly ground black pepper	

1 In bowl of blender or food processor fitted with a steel blade, combine sun-dried tomatoes, red pepper, mustard, garlic, vinegar, and onion. Process 30 seconds, or until tomatoes are ground.
2 Slowly drizzle in oils in a thin stream. Season with salt and pepper to taste.

For a cool, light, summer evening meal, pour this dressing over cooked green and white tortellini and you'll have a simple, yet elegant pasta salad.

SWEET AND SOUR DRESSING

Yield: Approximately 1⅓ cups (325 mL)

The unusual yet marvelous combination of honey and onion perks up the taste buds.

⅓ cup	cider vinegar	75 mL
⅓ cup	honey	75 mL
2 tablespoons	finely diced onion	25 mL
1	small clove garlic, minced	1
⅔ cup	corn or safflower oil	150 mL
1 teaspoon	dried oregano	5 mL
	Salt	
	Freshly ground black pepper	

1 In bowl of blender or food processor fitted with a steel blade, combine vinegar, honey, onion, and garlic. Process 30 seconds, or until smooth.
2 With machine running, drizzle in oil until combined. Stir in oregano. Season with salt and pepper to taste.

This dressing will banish boredom from your everyday tossed salad. Try it with a combination of chunks of leaf and iceberg lettuces, sliced radishes, peppers, green onions, and cherry tomatoes.

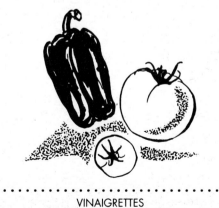

TOMATO CAPER DRESSING

Yield: Approximately 1¹/₄ cups (300 mL)

Tomatoes and capers make a perfect summertime combination. Just ask the southern Italians.

1 tablespoon	tomato paste	15 mL
1 teaspoon	Dijon-style mustard	5 mL
1	clove garlic, minced	1
1 teaspoon	honey	5 mL
¹/₄ cup	red wine vinegar	50 mL
¹/₄ cup	olive oil	50 mL
¹/₄ cup	basil oil or 1 tablespoon (15 mL) fresh or dried basil with ¹/₄ cup (50 mL) safflower or corn oil	50 mL
1	medium tomato, finely chopped	1
2 teaspoons	capers, finely chopped	10 mL
	Salt	
	Freshly ground black pepper	

1 In a small bowl, whisk together tomato paste, mustard, garlic, honey, and vinegar until combined.
2 While continuing to whisk, drizzle in oils in a very thin stream. Add tomato and capers and season with salt and pepper to taste. For best results, refrigerate about 1 hour before serving to allow flavors to combine.

Pour this dressing over steamed globe artichokes and let marinate for a couple of hours before regaling.

For a cooked vegetable salad, the flavor of the dressing is best absorbed if tossed over warm vegetables.

TOMATO WALNUT DRESSING

Yield: Approximately ²/₃ cup (150 mL)

Another taste bud-stimulating concoction by California caterer George Dolese. The combination of thyme and tomato makes this dressing truly special.

¹/₄ cup	tomato sauce	50 mL
¹/₄ cup	red wine vinegar	50 mL
1	medium clove garlic, minced	1
1 tablespoon	finely chopped fresh thyme leaves	15 mL
2 tablespoons	walnut oil	25 mL
¹/₂ cup	olive oil	125 mL
	Salt	
	Freshly ground white pepper	

1 In a bowl, whisk together tomato sauce, vinegar, garlic, and thyme until combined.
2 While continuing to whisk, slowly drizzle in oils. Season with salt and pepper to taste.

George suggests serving this dressing over a salad of cooked fusilli pasta, pink lentils, and basil, or on a salad of couscous, chunks of French feta cheese, diced English cucumbers, yellow pear tomatoes, and sliced scallions.

FOUR

MAYONNAISES

No other creamy sauce can compare to a homemade mayonnaise, but the creation of this perfect sauce has daunted many an otherwise adventuresome cook.

Just remember, don't bother even attempting a mayonnaise if a thunderstorm is forecast or is in progress, or if it's a hot, humid summer day. It simply won't bind. Instead, resort to your favorite bottled brand.

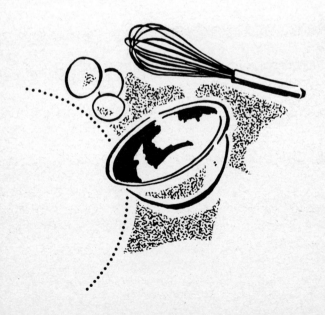

QUICK
MAYONNAISE

Yield: Approximately 1 cup (250 mL)

This mayonnaise recipe produces a thick creamy variety. If you want
to use it for a salad dressing, I suggest thinning it with 2 teaspoons
(10 mL) whipping cream or cold water. The cream will give a
wonderful rich concoction, and the water will give a little less
fattening variety. All variations may also be thinned.

1	large egg, at room temperature if possible	1
2 tablespoons	lemon juice or juice of $^1/_2$ a lemon	25 mL
1 teaspoon	Dijon-style mustard	5 mL
1 cup	safflower or corn oil, at room temperature if possible	250 mL
	Salt	
	Freshly ground white pepper	
2 teaspoons	whipping cream (35%) or cold water (optional)	10 mL

1 In bowl of blender or food processor fitted with a steel blade,
   combine egg, lemon juice, and mustard. Process 5 seconds, or until
   blended.
2 With machine running, gradually drizzle in oil through feed tube
   until thickened. Season with salt and pepper to taste.
3 For a thinner dressing whisk in cream or cold water.
4 Store mayonnaise in a covered container in the refrigerator for up
   to 5 days.

If your mayonnaise should refuse to thicken or appears curdled, don't
throw it out. Set it aside. Clean and dry the blender or food processor
bowl. Add a new egg yolk, 1 teaspoon (5 mL) Dijon-style mustard, and
1 tablespoon (15 mL) of your unsuccessful sauce. While the machine is
running, slowly drizzle in the failed sauce until you've achieved a
thick, creamy mayonnaise.

HERB
MAYONNAISE

Yield: Approximately ³/₄ cup (175 mL)

³/₄ cup	Quick Mayonnaise (page 55)	175 mL
2 tablespoons	finely chopped fresh parsley	25 mL
1 tablespoon	finely chopped fresh chives	15 mL
1 tablespoon	finely chopped tarragon or 1 teaspoon (5 mL) dried	15 mL
1 tablespoon	finely chopped chervil	15 mL
2 teaspoons	whipping cream (35%) or cold water (optional)	10 mL

1 Combine all ingredients and chill 2 hours to allow flavors to enhance. For a thinner dressing, whisk in cream or water.

Herb Mayonnaise is wonderful as a sauce for cold poached fish. Thin it with cream or water and use it as your everyday creamy dressing over tossed greens.

HORSERADISH
CRÈME

Yield: Approximately 1¼ cups (300 mL)

1 cup	Quick Mayonnaise (page 55)	250 mL
¼ cup	whipping cream (35%), whipped until stiff	50 mL
3 tablespoons	freshly grated horseradish or drained bottled horseradish	50 mL
1 teaspoon	finely grated lemon rind	5 mL

1 Combine all ingredients. Chill until serving.

Be sure to serve this creamy sauce at your traditional roast beef dinners. It complements the meat perfectly.

MUSTARD
MAYONNAISE

Yield: Approximately 1 cup (250 mL)

³/₄ cup	Quick Mayonnaise (page 55)	175 mL
¹/₄ cup	whipping cream (35%), whipped until stiff	50 mL
2 tablespoons	Dijon-style mustard	25 mL

1 Combine all ingredients. Chill until serving.

I love to serve this creamy and mildly hot sauce with slices of cold roast beef and lots of fried red onions.

REMOULADE

Yield: Approximately 1 cup (250 mL)

2	anchovy fillets packed in oil, drained	2
1 cup	Quick Mayonnaise (page 55)	250 mL
1 tablespoon	finely chopped gherkins (about 2 medium)	15 mL
1 tablespoon	finely chopped fresh parsley	15 mL
2 teaspoons	Dijon-style mustard	10 mL
2 teaspoons	finely chopped capers	10 mL
1 teaspoon	finely chopped tarragon or ¼ teaspoon (1 mL) dried	5 mL
1 teaspoon	finely chopped chervil or ¼ teaspoon (1 mL) dried	5 mL

1 Combine all ingredients. Refrigerate until serving.

This dressing makes an excellent dip for deep-fried seafood. But try it as a side sauce for cold roast pork, beef, or chicken, too.

TARTAR MAYONNAISE

Yield: Approximately 1 cup (250 mL)

2	medium shallots, finely diced	2
1	large egg, hard boiled and finely diced	1
3/4 cup	Quick Mayonnaise (page 55)	175 mL
1 tablespoon	minced gherkins (about 2 medium)	15 mL
1 tablespoon	finely chopped capers	15 mL
1 tablespoon	finely chopped parsley	15 mL
1 teaspoon	finely chopped fresh tarragon or 1/4 teaspoon (1 mL) dried	5 mL

1 Combine all ingredients. Refrigerate until serving.

Elegant when served with gougonettes of sole or simple when served with English-style battered fish and chips.

WATERCRESS MAYONNAISE

Yield: Approximately 1¹/4 cups (300 mL)

³/4 cup	watercress leaves, washed and dried, stems removed	175 mL
2 tablespoons	lemon juice	25 mL
1	large egg, at room temperature	1
1 teaspoon	Dijon-style mustard	5 mL
1 cup	safflower or corn oil	250 mL
	Salt	
	Freshly ground black pepper	
2 teaspoons	whipping cream (35%) or cold water (optional)	10 mL

1 In bowl of blender or food processor fitted with a steel blade, combine watercress and lemon juice. Process 30 seconds, or until smooth. Add egg and mustard and process another 5 seconds, or until blended.

2 With machine running, slowly drizzle in oil until thickened. Season with salt and pepper to taste. For a thinner dressing whisk in cream or water. Chill until serving.

Another wonderful flavored sauce. Pour it over cold fish, or try it on an elegant fish salad made with smoked trout and red and yellow pepper strips over Boston and Bibb lettuces.

AÏOLI

Yield: Approximately 1 cup (250 mL)

1	thin slice Italian or other white bread, crusts removed	1
3 tablespoons	milk	50 mL
4	medium cloves garlic, minced	4
2	large egg yolks	2
2 tablespoons	lemon juice	25 mL
¹/₂ cup	olive oil	125 mL
	Salt	
	Freshly ground white pepper	

1 In a small bowl, combine bread and milk. Let soak 5 minutes. Squeeze the bread with your hands to get rid of any excess liquid.

2 Place bread, garlic, egg yolks, and lemon juice in blender or food processor fitted with a steel blade. Process 10 seconds, or until completely smooth.

3 With machine running, slowly drizzle in oil until thickened. Season with salt and pepper to taste.

At a true Provençal feast, Aïoli is served with mounds of boiled vegetables — leeks, cauliflower, green beans — boiled eggs, poached flaky salt-cod, and crusty French bread. Or the dip may accompany sea snails or bourride — a Provençal fish stew.

Aïoli is a way of life in Provence. Certain days are set aside in the small villages for the Grand Aïoli — a feast that lasts from noon to sundown during which platters of food are passed around for dipping in the smooth garlicky delight.

VARIATIONS

ROUILLE Add 1 peeled, seeded, roasted red pepper to Aïoli recipe. Combine in blender or food processor with bread, garlic, egg yolks, and lemon juice. Follow the rest of the Aïoli recipe.

SKORDALIA Add ½ cup (125 mL) finely ground blanched almonds and 2 tablespoons (25 mL) chopped parsley to one Aïoli recipe. Stir to combine.

BRAISED, CREAMY
GARLIC DRESSING

Yield: Approximately 1¹/₃ cups (325 mL)

Roasting or braising garlic seems to mellow its flavor. You'll be surprised how light it can be, but you'll still be able to fight off the vampires.

6	medium cloves garlic	6
1	large egg, at room temperature if possible	1
2 teaspoons	Dijon-style mustard	10 mL
¹/₄ cup	lemon juice	50 mL
¹/₂ cup	peanut oil	125 mL
¹/₄ cup	olive oil	50 mL
¹/₄ cup	sour cream	50 mL
	Salt	
	Freshly ground white pepper	

1 Place garlic in a small saucepan, cover with water, and bring to a boil over medium-high heat. Reduce heat to low and simmer until tender, about 20 minutes. Remove from heat, strain, and cool to room temperature. Or, if you have the time, rub garlic cloves with 1 tablespoon (15 mL) butter and roast in a 350°F (180°C) oven until tender, about 20 to 30 minutes. Remove outer skin.

2 In bowl of blender or food processor fitted with a steel blade, combine garlic, egg, mustard, and lemon juice. Process 15 seconds, or until smooth. With machine running, slowly drizzle in oils in a very thin stream until thickened. Scrape into a bowl. Whisk in sour cream and season with salt and pepper to taste. Chill until serving.

For a variation, toss with finely grated celeriac or use on a spinach or green salad.

"Garlic is the catsup of intellectuals." — *Anonymous*

TRADITIONAL CAESAR DRESSING

Yield: Approximately ³/₄ cup (175 mL)

The traditional Caesar dressing is made with the salad greens.

2	cloves garlic	2
¹/₄ teaspoon	dry mustard	1 mL
1 teaspoon	Worcestershire sauce	5 mL
¹/₄ teaspoon	black pepper	1 mL
4	anchovies, minced	4
¹/₂ cup	olive oil	125 mL
1	egg yolk	1
1 head	romaine lettuce, torn in bite-size pieces	1 head
2-3 tablespoons	lemon juice or juice of ¹/₂ a lemon	25-50 mL
1 cup	croutons	250 mL
¹/₄ cup	freshly grated Parmesan cheese	50 mL

1 Crush 1 clove garlic and combine with mustard, Worcestershire sauce, pepper, anchovies, and oil. Refrigerate.
2 In a small saucepan bring 2 inches (5 cm) of water to a boil. Lower egg in water. Let stand 1 minute, and set aside to cool.
3 Cut remaining clove of garlic in half and rub it on the inside of a wooden bowl. Add romaine lettuce. Shake oil mixture and pour over lettuce. Separate egg and place egg yolk in center of salad. Pour lemon juice directly over egg yolk. Toss salad well. Sprinkle with croutons and Parmesan cheese and toss again.

CAESAR DRESSING

Yield: Approximately 1¹/₄ cups (300 mL)

I finally managed to twist my cousin Louise Lewis' arm for this recipe.
So Caesar lovers rejoice! You've finally found the imperial feast.

3	medium cloves garlic, minced	3
4	anchovy fillets packed in oil, drained	4
1 teaspoon	Dijon-style mustard	5 mL
1 tablespoon	chopped fresh parsley	15 mL
¹/₂ teaspoon	Worcestershire sauce	2 mL
3 tablespoons	white wine vinegar or lemon juice	50 mL
1	raw egg	1
¹/₄ teaspoon	black pepper	1 mL
3 tablespoons	freshly grated Parmesan cheese, preferably Parmigiano Reggiano	50 mL
¹/₂ cup	corn or safflower oil	125 mL
¹/₄ cup	olive oil	50 mL

1 In bowl of blender or food processor fitted with a steel blade,
   combine garlic, anchovies, mustard, parsley, Worcestershire sauce,
   vinegar or lemon juice, egg, pepper, and Parmesan cheese. Process
   30 seconds, or until smooth.
2 With machine running, slowly drizzle in oils in a thin stream. Be
   sure not to overbeat or dressing will become too thick.

You'll have enough dressing to coat 2 heads of romaine lettuce. Add
some homemade croutons and grate some more Parmesan cheese over
top.

*Parmigiano Reggiano: Reggiano is the king of Italian cheese and the
very essence of Italian cooking. Pale yellow and rock hard with a
thick brown rind, it's deceiving because it's soft and moist in the mouth.
Keeps best whole, wrapped in plastic.*

CURRY DRESSING

Yield: Approximately 1 cup (250 mL)

1 cup	Quick Mayonnaise (page 55)	250 mL
2 tablespoons	finely chopped mango chutney	25 mL
1 teaspoon	curry powder	5 mL
1/4 teaspoon	ground ginger or 3/4 teaspoon (3 mL) freshly grated ginger root	1 mL
2 teaspoons	whipping cream (35%) or cold water (optional)	10 mL

1 Combine all ingredients and chill until serving. If desired, dressing may be thinned by whisking in cream or water.

This dressing is perfect for a scrumptious cold rice salad or a chicken salad made with chunks of poached chicken, chopped dried apricots, celery, green onions, red pepper, and dried currants.

HORSERADISH AND CAPER DRESSING

Yield: Approximately 1¼ cups (300 mL)

My friend George Dolese has come up with another winner. His dressings and salads are featured at Neiman-Marcus in California.

1 cup	Quick Mayonnaise (page 55)	250 mL
2 tablespoons	prepared horseradish	25 mL
1 tablespoon	Dijon-style mustard	15 mL
1 tablespoon	capers	15 mL
	Salt	
	Freshly ground white pepper	

1 Place mayonnaise, horseradish, mustard, and capers in bowl of blender or food processor fitted with a steel blade. Process until smooth. Season with salt and pepper to taste.

George says this dressing is best suited for a cold potato salad or on cold roast beef, pork, or lamb.

OLD–FASHIONED THOUSAND ISLAND DRESSING

Yield: Approximately 2¹/₂ cups (625 mL)

The kind your grandmother used to make.

1	large egg	1
2 tablespoons	chili sauce	25 mL
1 tablespoon	lemon juice	15 mL
2 teaspoons	Dijon-style mustard	10 mL
1	medium tomato, peeled, seeded, and chopped (squeeze out excess liquid between hands)	1
1 cup	safflower or corn oil	250 mL
2	hard-boiled eggs, finely chopped	2
¹/₂ cup	sweet relish	125 mL
¹/₄ cup	sliced green onions	50 mL
	Salt	
	Freshly ground black pepper	

1 In bowl of blender or food processor fitted with a steel blade, combine egg, chili sauce, lemon juice, mustard, and tomato. Process 10 seconds, or until smooth.

2 With machine running, drizzle in oil in a very slow steady stream. Dressing should thicken slightly.

3 Transfer mixture to a bowl. Stir in eggs, relish, and onions. Season with salt and pepper to taste and refrigerate until use.

This one will dress up any plain tossed salad. But for something a little more unusual, pour it over either shrimp or crab on a bed of fresh spinach leaves with cherry tomatoes and homemade croutons.

To peel a tomato quickly: With a small paring knife, cut out its core and place an X on its bottom. Drop the tomato into boiling water and leave for 30 seconds. Remove with a slotted spoon and the skin will slip off easily.

TONNATO
DRESSING

Yield: Approximately 1³/₄ cups (425 mL)

4	anchovy fillets packed in oil, drained	4
1 tablespoon	Dijon-style mustard	15 mL
1	large egg	1
¹/₄ cup	lemon juice or juice of 1¹/₂ lemons	50 mL
3	medium cloves garlic, minced	3
1	can (6¹/₂ ounces/184 g) tuna, packed in oil	1
¹/₂ cup	corn or safflower oil	125 mL
¹/₄ cup	olive oil	50 mL
1 tablespoon	chopped capers	15 mL
	Salt	
	Freshly ground pepper	

1 In bowl of blender or food processor fitted with a steel blade, combine anchovies, mustard, egg, lemon juice, garlic, and half the tuna. Process 1 minute, or until smooth, scraping down sides occasionally.
2 With machine running, slowly drizzle in oils until thickened slightly.
3 Remove to small bowl. Stir in remaining tuna and capers. Season with salt and pepper to taste. Chill until serving.

This dressing is perfect for a Niçoise salad. Drizzle it over a platter of steamed green beans, hard-boiled eggs, black olives, tomato wedges, and boiled red-skinned potatoes.

FIVE

DAIRY-BASED DRESSINGS

Luscious and smooth, a rich-tasting sensation, could anything be more beautiful than a creamy dressing? This section will cover a number of these delights to unleash the flavors of your salads.

AVOCADO AND DILL DRESSING

Yield: Approximately 1 cup (250 mL)

The avocado is known as the love fruit. You'll understand why after you taste these dressings: you'll just love them.

1	ripe avocado	1
¼ cup	mayonnaise	50 mL
¼ cup	yogurt	50 mL
2 tablespoons	lemon or lime juice	25 mL
1 teaspoon	chopped fresh dill	5 mL
	Salt	
	Freshly ground white pepper	
2 tablespoons	milk (optional)	25 mL

1 In bowl of blender or food processor fitted with a steel blade, combine all ingredients. Process until smooth. Chill until serving. If you want to thin dressing, whisk in 2 tablespoons (25 mL) milk.

For a mouth-watering salad, drizzle Avocado and Dill Dressing on a spinach salad with thinly sliced water chestnuts, tomato wedges, and toasted almonds.

VARIATION

GUACAMOLE DRESSING Place avocado, mayonnaise, yogurt, and lemon juice in blender and process until smooth. Stir in ½ cup (125 mL) finely diced, seeded tomato, 1 tablespoon (15 mL) chopped fresh cilantro (or coriander), salt and pepper to taste, and ⅛ teaspoon (0.5 mL) hot pepper sauce. If you want to thin dressing, whisk in 2 tablespoons (25 mL) milk.

Guacamole Dressing is wonderful over a warm Mexican salad with nacho chips, warm chili, lots of shredded lettuce, chopped tomatoes, and grated Cheddar cheese.

CREAMY BLUE CHEESE, ROQUEFORT, OR GORGONZOLA DRESSING

Yield: Approximately 1⅓ cups (325 mL)

⅓ cup	Danish blue cheese, Roquefort, or Gorgonzola, crumbled	75 mL
2 tablespoons	white vinegar	25 mL
½ cup	mayonnaise	125 mL
½ cup	sour cream	125 mL
1 tablespoon	chopped fresh chives	15 mL
¼ teaspoon	dry mustard	1 mL
2-3 drops	Worcestershire sauce	2-3 drops
2 drops	tabasco sauce	2 drops
	Freshly ground white pepper	

1 In a small bowl, mash 4 tablespoons (50 mL) of the cheese with the vinegar. Once the mixture is fairly smooth, whisk in mayonnaise, sour cream, chives, mustard, Worcestershire sauce, and tabasco sauce. Season with pepper to taste. Add remaining cheese and chill until serving.

2 If dressing thickens in the refrigerator, thin with additional sour cream.

Drizzle this dressing over a combination of chilled iceberg lettuce, watercress, cucumber slices, and tomato wedges.

CREAMY CUCUMBER DRESSING

Yield: Approximately 1 cup (250 mL)

A refreshing summer dressing!

¹/₂ cup	peeled, seeded, and coarsely grated cucumber (about ¹/₂ of a medium cucumber)	125 mL
¹/₄ teaspoon	salt	1 mL
¹/₂ cup	mayonnaise	125 mL
¹/₃ cup	sour cream or plain yogurt	75 mL
2 teaspoons	lemon juice	10 mL
¹/₂ teaspoon	granulated sugar	2 mL
2 teaspoons	chopped fresh dill	10 mL
	Salt	
	Freshly ground white pepper	

1 In a small sieve set over a bowl, toss the cucumber with the salt and let drain 10 minutes. Then squeeze cucumber in hands to remove any remaining liquid.
2 Meanwhile, in bowl of blender or food processor fitted with a steel blade, combine mayonnaise, sour cream or yogurt, lemon juice, sugar, and dill. Process 30 to 45 seconds, or until smooth. Add the cucumber and process until combined, about 5 seconds. Season with salt and pepper to taste. For best results, refrigerate mixture 1 to 2 hours to deepen flavors.

Try on a combination of curly endive, Boston lettuce, Bibb lettuce, and radicchio.

GREEN GODDESS DRESSING

Yield: Approximately 1⅓ cups (325 mL)

Sometimes the old-fashioned way really is the best — as in this dressing.

½ cup	low-calorie sour cream	125 mL
3 tablespoons	finely chopped fresh parsley	50 mL
4	anchovy fillets packed in oil, drained	4
1 tablespoon	finely chopped chives	15 mL
¼ cup	lemon juice or juice of 1¼ lemons	50 mL
1	small clove garlic, minced	1
1 teaspoon	finely chopped capers	5 mL
¾ cup	mayonnaise	175 mL
	Salt	
	White pepper	

1 In bowl of blender or food processor fitted with a steel blade, combine sour cream, parsley, anchovies, chives, lemon juice, garlic, and capers. Process 30 seconds, or until smooth, scraping down sides occasionally.
2 Remove to a small bowl. Whisk in mayonnaise and season with salt and pepper to taste. Chill until serving.

For a creamy delight, drizzle this dressing on a combination of greens like arugula and Boston, Bibb, and romaine lettuces with sliced radishes, celery, green pepper, and cherry tomatoes.

JAMES' EASY CREAMY DRESSING

Yield: Approximately ²/₃ cup (150 mL)

My friend James developed this marvelous concoction. It's wonderful, easy, and elegant.

²/₃ cup	sour cream or light (low-calorie) sour cream	150 mL
5 teaspoons	lemon juice	25 mL
1 tablespoon	honey	15 mL
	Salt	
	Freshly ground white pepper	

1 In a small bowl, whisk together all ingredients. Chill until serving.

This dressing perfectly complements a salad of cooked shrimp served over either slices of avocado and papaya or a variety of mixed greens.

LEMON GOAT CHEESE DRESSING

Yield: Approximately 1 cup (250 mL)

The lemon flavor adds a ray of freshness to any salad.

1/4 cup	young or mild goat cheese, crumbled	50 mL
2 tablespoons	lemon juice	25 mL
1 tablespoon	finely grated lemon rind	15 mL
1/2 cup	mayonnaise	125 mL
1/3 cup	sour cream	75 mL
2 tablespoons	chopped fresh chives	25 mL
1	small clove garlic, minced	1
3 tablespoons	light cream	50 mL
1/2 teaspoon	coarsely ground black pepper	2 mL
	Salt	

1   In a small bowl, whisk together goat cheese and lemon juice until fairly smooth. Whisk in lemon rind, mayonnaise, sour cream, chives, and garlic.
2   While continuing to whisk, drizzle in cream until desired consistency. Season with pepper and salt to taste. Chill until serving.
3   If dressing thickens in the refrigerator, thin with additional cream.

For a beautiful, fresh appetizer, toss this dressing with blanched fiddleheads and spoon into radicchio cups; or pour over steamed green beans or on a combination of greens.

OLD–FASHIONED BOILED DRESSING

Yield: Approximately 1³/₄ cups (425 mL)

Recipe tester Karen Tufford-Brehn was kind enough to share this old Tufford family recipe.

³/₄ cup	granulated sugar	175 mL
1 tablespoon	cornstarch	15 mL
1 teaspoon	dry mustard	5 mL
1 teaspoon	salt	5 mL
3	large eggs, beaten well	3
1 cup	white vinegar	250 mL
1 teaspoon	butter	5 mL
	whipping cream (35%) (optional)	

1 In a bowl, combine sugar, cornstarch, mustard, and salt. Stir in eggs until smooth.
2 Meanwhile, in a medium-sized saucepan, bring vinegar just to a boil over medium-high heat. Whisk in egg mixture until smooth. Continue cooking, whisking constantly, until thickened. Remove from heat. Stir in butter. Cool. Mixture can be thinned with cream.

Karen's Grandma Hills liked to use this dressing on a potato salad, coleslaw, or over hard-boiled egg halves.

RANCH–STYLE DRESSING

Yield: Approximately 1¼ cups (300 mL)

I've always loved bottled Ranch dressings and have searched high and low for a recipe. This recipe is my version. But where did it get the name Ranch-style?

½ cup	mayonnaise	125 mL
⅓ cup	sour cream	75 mL
⅓ cup	buttermilk	75 mL
1	small clove garlic, minced	1
2 tablespoons	finely chopped fresh parsley	25 mL
1 tablespoon	chopped fresh chives	15 mL
½ teaspoon	Dijon-style mustard	2 mL
⅛ teaspoon	celery seed	0.5 mL
⅛ teaspoon	onion powder	0.5 mL
Pinch	dried marjoram	Pinch
2 drops	Worcestershire sauce	2 drops
	Salt	
	Freshly ground white pepper	

1 In a bowl, whisk mayonnaise and sour cream until smooth. Whisking continuously, slowly pour in buttermilk until combined. Add remaining ingredients and chill until serving.

Cleopatra used buttermilk as a beauty mask and some say it fades freckles. It's necessary in making crème fraiche and is only slightly more caloric than a glass of skim milk.

SIX

WARM DRESSINGS

For a striking contrast in flavor and texture, warm dressings are often served on uncooked, room-temperature ingredients. A warm dressing tossed over sturdy leaves like cabbage, chicory, and dandelion greens helps to break down the coarse fibers. This process is called *wilting*. Use these warm salad dressings to create new, unusual salad sensations.

INDONESIAN PEANUT DRESSING

Yield: Approximately 1½ cups (375 mL)

⅓ cup	crunchy peanut butter	75 mL
1 tablespoon	finely grated ginger root	15 mL
1	small clove garlic, minced	1
2 tablespoons	Indonesian sweet soy sauce or dark soy sauce	25 mL
¼ cup	rice vinegar	50 mL
1 tablespoon	honey	15 mL
¾ cup	unsweetened coconut milk	175 mL
1 teaspoon	chili oil or more to taste	5 mL
¼ teaspoon	sesame oil or more to taste	1 mL
	Chicken stock or water (optional)	

1 In a small bowl, whisk together peanut butter, ginger root, garlic, soy sauce, rice vinegar, and honey until smooth.

2 Slowly whisk in coconut milk and season with chili and sesame oils. If dressing is too thick, thin with chicken stock or water. Serve dressing at room temperature or warm over low heat.

Toss this dressing over a salad of shredded poached chicken breasts, Chinese buckwheat noodles, sliced, peeled, and seeded cucumbers, bean sprouts, and sliced green onions.

MUSTARD CARAWAY DRESSING

Yield: Approximately 1 cup (250 mL)

½ cup	olive oil	125 mL
1 tablespoon	red wine vinegar	15 mL
1	clove garlic, minced	1
¼ cup	finely diced red onion	50 mL
2 tablespoons	Dijon-style mustard	25 mL
¼ cup	chopped fresh parsley	50 mL
2 tablespoons	caraway seeds	25 mL
	Salt	
	Freshly ground white pepper	

1 Combine oil, vinegar, garlic, and onion in a small saucepan over medium-high heat. Bring just to a boil. Remove from heat. Whisk in mustard. Add parsley and caraway seeds. Season with salt and pepper to taste. Use immediately.

For a tantalizing treat, toss this dressing over still-warm, halved, baby, red-skinned potatoes.

WARM AND CREAMY BACON DRESSING

Yield: Approximately 1¹/₃ cups (325 mL)

3	rashers bacon	3
	(about 4 ounces/100 g)	
¹/₂ cup	coarsely chopped pecans	125 mL
1 tablespoon	all-purpose flour	15 mL
1 cup	sour cream	250 mL
2 tablespoons	cider vinegar	25 mL
2 teaspoons	roasted pecan oil or	10 mL
	walnut oil	
2 teaspoons	honey	10 mL
	Salt	
	White pepper	

1 In a medium-sized heavy skillet, fry bacon over medium heat until crisp. Remove with a slotted spoon, crumble, and set aside.
2 Add pecans to skillet and cook 4 minutes, or until golden. Remove with a slotted spoon and set aside.
3 Whisk flour into bacon fat and cook about 1 minute, or until bubbling slightly. Whisk in sour cream, vinegar, oil, and honey. Cook 1 to 2 minutes, whisking constantly. Return bacon and nuts to skillet. Season with salt and pepper to taste. Serve immediately.

For a perfect appetizer, toss this warm and creamy dressing over Belgian endive or a combination of bitter greens like arugula and radicchio.

WARM BACON AND
MOLASSES DRESSING

Yield: Approximately 1 cup (250 mL)

The combination of smoky bacon and molasses gives this dressing a
down-home, southern, country flavor.

3	rashers bacon (about 4 ounces/100 g), finely chopped	3
2	small shallots, finely chopped	2
1	medium clove garlic, minced	1
1/2 teaspoon	dried thyme or 1 1/2 teaspoons (7 mL) fresh thyme	2 mL
1/4 cup	red wine vinegar	50 mL
2 tablespoons	light molasses	25 mL
1/4 cup	safflower or corn oil	50 mL
	Cayenne pepper	
	Salt	
	Freshly ground black pepper	

1 In a heavy skillet, sauté bacon over medium-high heat until golden,
   about 4 minutes.
2 Add shallots, garlic, and thyme and sauté 2 minutes, or until
   shallots are wilted slightly. Whisk in vinegar and molasses and
   bring to a boil.
3 Remove from heat. While whisking continuously, slowly drizzle in
   oil in a thin stream until thickened slightly. Season with cayenne,
   salt, and pepper to taste. Use immediately.

Pour warm dressing over a fall main dish salad of grilled chicken
chunks and grilled red, green, and yellow peppers cut into julienne
strips, or drizzle over a spinach and escarole salad with lots of sliced
mushrooms, parboiled red-skinned potato slices, and red onion rings.
Or for a warm potato salad, drizzle over warm red-skinned potato
halves.

SEVEN

LOW-CALORIE DRESSINGS

Sometimes the temptation is just too much and we succumb to a piece of rich chocolate cake with ice cream or our mothers' strawberry-rhubarb crumble. As we all know, these indulgences play havoc with our calorie count — not to mention what they do to our conscience. But not to worry! Leafy green vegetable and broiled meat salads are the perfect diet foods, as long as they are prepared without rich dressings.

This section offers a number of wonderful-tasting, low-calorie dressings to let you forget you're on a calorie budget.

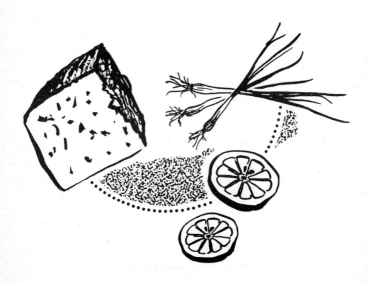

CRANBERRY COOLER DRESSING

Yield: Approximately ¹/₂ cup (125 mL)
Calorie Count: 38 calories per tablespoon (15 mL)

The refreshing, fruity taste of cranberries makes this dressing a real taste sensation.

¹/₄ cup	low-calorie cranberry juice	50 mL
2 tablespoons	cider vinegar	25 mL
2 tablespoons	peanut oil	25 mL
1 tablespoon	finely chopped shallot or onion	15 mL
1 teaspoon	honey	5 mL

1 Combine all ingredients in a screw-top jar. Shake vigorously. Refrigerate 1 hour to allow flavors to enhance.
2 Bring back to room temperature before serving, since refrigerated oil thickens.

To make your salad a more interesting treat, use unusual greens like arugula, combined with Boston and romaine lettuces. Add sliced red onion, yellow pepper, and cucumber and sprinkle with chopped hard-boiled egg whites.

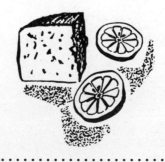

CREAMY GARLIC DRESSING

Yield: Approximately 1 cup (250 mL)
Calorie Count: 16 calories per tablespoon (15 mL)

Low-fat yogurt adds a creamy, rich texture to your dressing with scarcely any fat. Eat some parsley afterwards as the chlorophyll wards off the garlic odor.

1 cup	plain low-fat yogurt	250 mL
2 tablespoons	low-calorie mayonnaise	25 mL
1 teaspoon	Dijon-style mustard	5 mL
2	large cloves garlic, minced	2
	Salt	
	Freshly ground white pepper	

1 In a small bowl, whisk together all ingredients until smooth. Refrigerate 1 to 2 hours to allow flavors to develop.

This low-calorie dressing is equally good as a dip for vegetables or dolloped on baked potatoes.

CREAMY RICOTTA DRESSING

Yield: Approximately ½ cup (125 mL)
Calorie Count: 37 calories per tablespoon (15 mL)

There's no joy in dieting, but if you have a few favorite low-calorie stand-by recipes like this creamy delight, you can usually make it through the difficult times.

½ cup	Ricotta cheese	125 mL
1	small clove garlic, minced	1
3	anchovy fillets packed in oil, drained	3
1 teaspoon	Dijon-style mustard	5 mL
¼ cup	lemon juice or juice of 1¼ lemons	50 mL
2 tablespoons	skim milk	25 mL
1 tablespoon	finely chopped fresh basil or 1 teaspoon (5 mL) dried basil	15 mL
1 teaspoon	finely chopped fresh chives	5 mL
1 teaspoon	chopped capers	5 mL
	Salt	
	White pepper	

1 In bowl of blender or food processor fitted with a steel blade, place cheese, garlic, anchovies, mustard, lemon juice, and milk. Process 1 minute, or until smooth, scraping down sides occasionally.
2 Stir in basil, chives, and capers. Add salt and pepper to taste. For best results, refrigerate 1 to 2 hours to allow flavors to blend.
3 If dressing thickens in the refrigerator, it can be thinned by adding 2 to 3 tablespoons (25 to 50 mL) skim milk.

For a perfect light luncheon, drizzle this creamy dressing over vine-ripened beefsteak tomatoes and sliced sweet onions.

DILL
DRESSING

Yield: Approximately ¹/₂ cup (125 mL)
Calorie Count: 23 calories per tablespoon (15 mL)
30 calories per tablespoon (15 mL)
with Parmesan

The refreshing taste of dill offers a summer treat all year long.

¹/₂ cup	plain low-fat yogurt	125 mL
2 tablespoons	reduced-calorie mayonnaise	25 mL
2 tablespoons	snipped fresh dill or	25 mL
	1 teaspoon (5 mL) dried dill	
	weed	
1 tablespoon	finely sliced green onions	15 mL
¹/₂ teaspoon	honey	2 mL
	Salt	
	Freshly ground white pepper	
2 tablespoons	freshly grated Parmesan	25 mL
	cheese (optional)	

1 In a small bowl, whisk together all ingredients. Chill 1 to 2 hours
to allow flavors to develop.

HONEY RICOTTA DRESSING

Yield: Approximately ³/₄ cup (175 mL)
Calorie Count: 20 calories per tablespoon (15 mL)

For a wonderful dessert, drizzle over a fruit salad. You'd never believe it's a healthy low-calorie treat.

¹/₂ cup	Ricotta cheese	125 mL
¹/₄ cup	skim milk	50 mL
3 tablespoons	lime juice	50 mL
2 tablespoons	honey	25 mL
¹/₄ teaspoon	ground cardamom (optional)	1 mL

1 Whisk together all ingredients. Chill until serving.

Ricotta, being the mild cheese that it is, blends beautifully with almost anything. Cardamom is best suited for fruit salads made with peaches, apricots, green apples, and grapes.

Cardamom: It is also called cardamon. A native to India and an important ingredient in Indian cuisine, cardamom is one of the more expensive spices because the pods must be hand-picked. These pods come in both white and green colors; the green is considered preferable. Each pod holds a number of small black seeds that contain the unusual, spicy flavor. The spice also comes ground.

Ricotta Cheese: A creamy, mild-flavored, almost sweet cheese, true Italian ricotta is made from the whey of Percorico cheese or from sheep's buttermilk. American-made ricotta is from skimmed cow's milk.

LOW–CALORIE MAYONNAISE

Yield: Approximately 1¹/₃ cups (325 mL)
Calorie Count: 22 calories per tablespoon (15 mL)

This surprisingly wonderful, low-calorie mayonnaise acts as a perfect substitute for the "real thing." It was developed by New York food writer Paul Piccuito, who has contributed to the Time/Life series, *Family Circle Magazine*, and *Weight Watchers Magazine*.

³/₄ cup	chicken broth	175 mL
1¹/₂ tablespoons	cornstarch, dissolved in 2 tablespoons (25 mL) cold water	20 mL
1	large egg, at room temperature if possible	1
3 tablespoons	lemon juice	50 mL
2 teaspoons	Dijon-style mustard	10 mL
1¹/₂ tablespoons	safflower oil	20 mL
	Salt	
	Freshly ground white pepper	

1 In a small saucepan, bring chicken broth to a boil over medium-high heat. Whisk in cornstarch mixture and bring back to a boil, whisking constantly. Continue to cook 1 minute, or until thickened. Remove from heat and cool to room temperature.

2 In bowl of blender or food processor fitted with a steel blade, place cooled chicken broth, egg, lemon juice, mustard, and oil. Process until smooth, about 30 seconds. Scrape into a small bowl, season with salt and pepper to taste, and chill until ready to serve.

ORIENTAL DRESSING

Yield: Approximately ³/₄ cup (175 mL)
Calorie Count: 45 calories per tablespoon (15 mL)

2	cloves garlic, minced	2
¹/₄ cup	rice wine vinegar	50 mL
¹/₄ cup	chicken stock	50 mL
3 tablespoons	peanut oil	50 mL
4 teaspoons	reduced-sodium soy sauce	20 mL
2 teaspoons	honey	10 mL
2 teaspoons	sesame oil	10 mL
1 teaspoon	freshly grated ginger root	5 mL

1 Combine all ingredients in a screw-top jar. Shake vigorously. Refrigerate 1 hour to allow flavors to enhance.
2 Be sure to bring dressing back to room temperature before serving because chicken stock may thicken.

This unusual dressing makes a lovely Oriental chicken salad. Combine chunks of poached chicken, bean sprouts, slices of red pepper, blanched broccoli, and melon chunks. Toss with dressing and serve in a melon half.

LOW-CALORIE
RANCH-STYLE DRESSING

Yield: Approximately 1¼ cups (300 mL)
Calorie Count: 36 calories per tablespoon (15 mL)

½ cup	low-calorie mayonnaise	125 mL
⅓ cup	low-calorie sour cream	75 mL
⅓ cup	buttermilk	75 mL
1	small clove garlic, minced	1
2 tablespoons	finely chopped fresh parsley	25 mL
1 tablespoon	chopped fresh chives	15 mL
½ teaspoon	Dijon-style mustard	2 mL
⅛ teaspoon	celery seed	0.5 mL
⅛ teaspoon	onion powder	0.5 mL
2 drops	Worcestershire sauce	2 drops
Pinch	dried marjoram	Pinch
	Salt	
	Freshly ground white pepper	

1 In a bowl, whisk mayonnaise and sour cream until smooth. Whisking continuously, slowly pour in buttermilk until combined.

2 Add remaining ingredients and chill until serving.

TOFU
DRESSING

Yield: Approximately 1 cup (250 mL)
Calorie Count: 19 calories per tablespoon (15 mL)

8 ounces	tofu, drained, about 1 cup (250 mL)	227 g
2 tablespoons	lemon juice	25 mL
2 teaspoons	Dijon-style mustard	10 mL
2 tablespoons	corn or safflower oil	25 mL
1/2 tablespoon	chopped fresh chives	7 mL
1/2 teaspoon	chopped fresh chervil	2 mL
1/2 teaspoon	chopped fresh tarragon	2 mL
	Salt	
	Freshly ground white pepper	

1 In bowl of blender or food processor fitted with a steel blade, combine tofu, lemon juice, and mustard. Process 15 seconds, or until smooth, scraping down sides occasionally.
2 With machine running, slowly drizzle in oil. Add remaining ingredients. Season with salt and pepper to taste.

For a low-calorie luncheon, spoon Tofu Dressing over a salad of mixed greens, blanched asparagus spears, and wedges of pink grapefruit. Or turn the dressing into an interesting dip for crudités (raw vegetables) by adding 2 tablespoons (25 mL) chopped fresh herbs — tarragon, basil, chives, chervil — and 1 or 2 cloves garlic, minced.

Tofu: Tofu is the Japanese name for bean curd — an inexpensive, low-calorie, non-animal source of protein. Its mild flavor makes it an ideal ingredient to combine with more flavorful foods.

WARM SICHUAN PEPPERCORN DRESSING

Yield: Approximately ²/₃ cup (150 mL)
Calorie Count: 13 calories per tablespoon (15 mL)

You'll never believe that this warm dressing is low in calories. Try it on a main dish salad when you're trimming down for summer.

1 teaspoon	peanut oil	5 mL
1	clove garlic, minced	1
1 inch	piece ginger root, finely grated	2.5 cm
3	green onions, finely sliced	3
¹/₂ tablespoon	crushed Sichuan peppercorns	7 mL
¹/₂ cup	chicken stock	125 mL
1 tablespoon	soy sauce	15 mL
2 tablespoons	rice vinegar	25 mL
¹/₄ teaspoon	orange chili oil or chili oil (or more to taste)	1 mL

1   Heat oil in a heavy skillet over medium-high heat. Add garlic, ginger root, onions, and peppercorns. Sauté 2 minutes, or until onions wilt slightly, stirring constantly.
2   Stir in stock, soy sauce, vinegar, and chili oil. Bring just to a boil and serve immediately.

Toss this warm dressing over thin strips of grilled New York strip steak, blanched snow peas, and baby corn. Or spoon it on Bibb lettuce and sprinkle with sesame seeds.

Sichuan Peppercorns: These reddish-brown peppercorns are native to the Sichuan province of China and are basic to its spicy cuisine, but they do not give off a palate-scorching hotness. If they are unavailable, black peppercorns can be used as an alternative.

EIGHT

FRUIT SALAD DESSERT DRESSINGS

Chocolate mousse, crème caramel, trifle, carrot cake, strawberry custard tarte — an elegant dessert will be remembered long after the meal has ended. Can a fruit salad ever really compete? In this section, you will discover dessert dressings that will complement the delicate flavor and succulence of the aristocratic dessert designed with fruit.

CARIBBEAN BANANA DRESSING

Yield: Approximately 1 cup (250 mL)

A visit to New York is not complete without the blender drinks I share with my friends Paul Piccuito and Michael Pavlicin. This dressing was inspired by one of those special fruity drinks.

1	very ripe banana	1
¹/₄ cup	unsweetened coconut milk	50 mL
3 tablespoons	dark rum or more	50 mL
2 tablespoons	lime juice	25 mL
2 tablespoons	honey	25 mL
	Freshly grated nutmeg	

1   In bowl of blender or food processor fitted with a steel blade, combine all ingredients. Process until smooth. Chill until serving.

Toss this dressing over a salad of sliced blood oranges and fresh pineapple and garnish with toasted coconut.

CREAMY ORANGE AND STRAWBERRY DESSERT DRESSING

Yield: Approximately 2 cups (500 mL)

3 cups	sliced strawberries	750 mL
³/₄ cup	freshly squeezed orange juice	175 mL
¹/₄ cup	orange-flavored liqueur	50 mL
¹/₄ cup	whipping cream (35%)	50 mL
3 tablespoons	orange blossom or other honey	50 mL

1 In bowl of blender or food processor fitted with a steel blade, combine strawberries and orange juice. Process until completely smooth. Press through a sieve with medium-sized holes into a bowl. Stir in liqueur, cream, and honey.

Drizzle this creamy delight over any combination fruit salad. It's also particularly nice over a combination melon salad.

ORANGE CREAM DRESSING

Yield: Approximately 2 cups (500 mL)

The orange flavor in this dressing will help you create a salad streaked with sunshine.

1 cup	plain yogurt	250 mL
1 cup	sour cream	250 mL
¼ cup	orange blossom or other honey	50 mL
2 tablespoons	frozen orange juice concentrate	25 mL
2 tablespoons	grated orange zest (about 1 orange)	25 mL
1 tablespoon	lemon juice	15 mL

1 In a small bowl, whisk together all ingredients. Chill before serving.

Drizzle the chilled dressing over blackberries or a combination of sliced peaches and wild blueberries.

FRUIT SALAD DESSERT DRESSINGS

SWEET ROSEMARY AND LEMON DRESSING

Yield: Approximately ¹/₂ cup (125 mL)

¹/₄ cup	honey	50 mL
¹/₄ cup	lemon juice	50 mL
1 teaspoon	fresh rosemary, slightly bruised, or dried rosemary	5 mL

1 In a small bowl, whisk together all ingredients. Let sit about 1 hour so rosemary flavor is enhanced.

Toss this refreshing dressing over a combination fruit salad. Rosemary blends well with the fall flavors of apples, pears, and other harvest fruits.

SUGGESTED DRESSINGS

BEEF SALADS

Guacamole Dressing
Horseradish and Caper Dressing
Horseradish Crème
Mexican-style Salsa Dressing
Mustard Mayonnaise
Spicy Indian Dressing
Warm Sichuan Peppercorn
   Dressing

CHICKEN SALADS

Curry Dressing
Indonesian Peanut Dressing
Oriental Dressing
   (low calorie)
Remoulade
Spicy Indian Dressing
Warm Bacon and Molasses
   Dressing

FISH OR SEAFOOD

Aïoli
Herb Mayonnaise
James' Easy Creamy Dressing
Mexican-style Salsa Dressing
Old-fashioned Thousand Island
   Dressing
Remoulade

Tartar Mayonnaise
Tonnato Dressing
Watercress Mayonnaise

FRUITS

Caribbean Banana Dressing
   (dessert)
Creamy Orange and Strawberry
   Dessert Dressing
   (dessert)
Honey Ricotta Dressing
   (low-calorie dessert)
James' Easy Creamy Dressing
Orange Cream Dressing
   (dessert)
Quebec or Vermont Maple
   Vinaigrette
Sweet Rosemary and Lemon
   Dressing
   (dessert)

TOSSED GREEN SALADS

Avocado and Dill Dressing
Braised, Creamy Garlic Dressing
Caesar Dressing
Cheesey Greek Salad Dressing
Classic Vinaigrette
Cranberry Cooler Dressing
   (low calorie)

Creamy Blue Cheese, Roquefort,
  or Gorgonzola Dressing
Creamy Cucumber Dressing
Creamy Garlic Dressing
  (low calorie)
Creamy Ricotta Dressing
  (low calorie)
Creamy Vinaigrette
Dill Dressing
  (low calorie)
Green Goddess Dressing
Herb Vinaigrette
Honey Raspberry Vinaigrette
Mustard Vinaigrette
Old-fashioned Thousand Island
  Dressing
Orange Poppyseed Dressing
Pickled Ginger Vinaigrette
Port Walnut Dressing
Ranch-style Dressing
Ranch-style Dressing
  (low calorie)
Roquefort or Blue Cheese
  Vinaigrette
Sweet and Sour Dressing
Tarragon Vinaigrette
Traditional Caesar Dressing
Warm Bacon and Molasses
  Dressing
Warm and Creamy Bacon
  Dressing
Watercress Mayonnaise

PASTA SALADS

Black Bean and Tomato Dressing
Hoisen Dressing
Indonesian Peanut Dressing
Pesto Salad Dressing
Roasted Red Pepper and Chive
  Dressing
Sun-dried Tomato Dressing
Tomato Walnut Dressing

POTATO SALADS

Horseradish and Caper Dressing
Moorland Herb Dressing
Mustard Caraway Dressing
Tonnato Dressing
Warm Bacon and Molasses
  Dressing

RICE AND GRAINS

Curry Dressing
Lemon Coriander Dressing
Tomato Walnut Dressing

VEGETABLE SALADS

Aïoli
  (assorted vegetables)

Basil Oil
  (tomatoes)
Braised, Creamy Garlic Dressing
  (celeriac)
Creamy Ricotta Dressing
  (tomatoes) (low calorie)
Lemon Goat Cheese Dressing
  (fiddleheads, green beans)
Mexican-style Salsa Dressing
  (corn)

Old-fashioned Boiled Dressing
  (cabbage)
Pesto Salad Dressing
  (tomatoes)
Port Walnut Dressing
  (snap peas)
Tofu Dressing
  (assorted crudités) (low calorie)
Tomato Caper Dressing
  (artichokes)

INDEX

ADDITIONAL
RECIPES